COMMUNICATIONS
FOR
MANAGERS

COMMUNICATIONS FOR MANAGERS

A PRACTICAL HANDBOOK

Original text written by BT Employee Communications

The Industrial Society

First published in 1993 by
The Industrial Society
Robert Hyde House
48 Bryanston Square
London W1H 7LN
Telephone: 071–262 2401

Original text © British Telecommunications plc 1992
Additional text © The Industrial Society 1993
Typographical arrangement © The Industrial Society 1993

ISBN 1 85838 028 X

British Library Cataloguing-in-Publication Data.
A catalogue record for this book is available from the
British Library

Typeset by: Midlands Book Typesetting Company, Loughborough
Printed by: Lavenham Press
Cover design: Integra Communications

Text illustrations: Sophie Grillet

ACKNOWLEDGEMENTS

This book is derived from a series of leaflets written and produced by BT people for use in British Telecommunications plc. Particular thanks are due to Timothy Beecroft, Gordon Butler, Mac Farquhar, Rita Kluwe, Gordon Lipton, Brenda McAll, John Melmoth and Cliff Norris.

CONTENTS

INTRODUCTION

Organisations which seek to release the potential of people at work need to ensure that they equip managers with the skills and drills of communication. Managers who can master running team meetings, communicating performance or organisational change, listening to the team's ideas and the other subjects covered in this book will have many of the necessary skills.

This book was originally written for managers in BT to help them with the practical issues of how to communicate. The chapters were initially produced as separate booklets but such was their popularity that they were reissued in a combined book.

The Industrial Society believes in spreading best practice and in encouraging organisations to take advantage of ways that have been developed to allow people to give of their best to their work. On finding this excellent guide at BT, we decided that a guide which had proved so useful to so many BT managers would probably also be valued by managers elsewhere.

Jenny Davenport
Senior Consultant
The Industrial Society

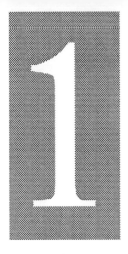

TEAM MEETINGS

Well-planned and well-run team meetings are essential for effective teamwork and contribute to business success.

Team meetings are a regular, timetabled opportunity for managers (team leaders) and their teams to discuss team performance and other issues.

There are a number of different ways of running team meetings. Some organisations use a strictly defined "team briefing" system; in others a more informal approach is adopted. Whichever approach is used, team meetings have proved to be popular and successful.

Face-to-face communication has a number of advantages over written methods:

- the opportunity exists for checking the team's understanding of the issues being discussed;

- the team has the chance to express views, concerns and questions to more senior managers, via the team leader;

- presenting information and issues to the whole team as a group increases the likelihood of achieving a unified team response;

- most people prefer face-to-face communication because it generates a sense of involvement and belonging.

Team meetings are the big employee communications success story of the past few years.

Successful team meetings are:

- regular;
- relevant;
- run by the team leader;
- monitored.

REGULAR

Each month, company-wide messages are agreed by the company's senior management forum and sent for briefing in team meetings. Within each division, information is cascaded through team meetings from the monthly board meeting (or equivalent) to everyone.

The dates of team meetings are set and diaried well in advance and not changed except in emergencies. Attendance at team meetings is mandatory for all team members and team leaders. Arrangements are made to brief, at a later date, any team members who miss a meeting owing to leave, sickness etc.

As far as possible, team meetings for each level in the organisation take place at the same time.

Team meetings focus on team performance information which is usually captured monthly. They are, therefore, an opportunity to review the past month's performance and focus on next month's targets. In effect, team meetings provide a forum for the discussion and implementation of quality issues, especially continuous improvement.

Where geographical constraints reduce the frequency of team meetings, alternative methods of communication are required to ensure timely delivery of information.

RELEVANT

Ensuring that the information presented at team meetings is relevant to the audience is crucial to the success of the system. Too often the mechanism is overloaded with non-urgent material simply because it is so effective a channel.

As well as team performance information and recognition of individual and team successes which, by definition, are always relevant to team members, team meetings are also used to communicate information from and about other parts of the organisation, the relevance of which is drawn out by the team leader. Second line and more senior managers ensure that their direct reports have sufficient background information to allow them to do this, without swamping them with detail.

In general, information, whether local or from the company as a whole, will fall into four categories:

- progress and performance;
- policy;
- people;
- points for action.

When delivering such information the emphasis should always be: "What does this mean to us and what do we need to do about it?"

More routine messages, which do not require changes to work practices, should be delivered through more appropriate channels – office notices, local newsletters, divisional publications etc.

RUN BY THE TEAM LEADER

Running team meetings highlights and reinforces the role of managers as leaders: it confirms them as their team's authoritative source of information and gives them the opportunity to act as the representative of the company as a whole to the team, and of the team to the company. Team leaders have the key role to play in managing the flow of feedback and upward communications.

Team leaders need the personal communications skills and management awareness necessary to deliver messages clearly, coherently and in a way that makes them relevant to the team. Training in these skills is available from The Industrial Society and can be delivered locally at the workplace or centrally.

Team leaders get answers to team questions and highlight team concerns by referring them up the management chain. A formal requirement to record questions and views expressed helps the team leader to discharge this responsibility.

Team leaders ensure that a member of their team is able to act in their place at any team meetings that they are unable to attend themselves.

MONITORED

Regular monitoring of the team meeting system as a whole will help to ensure that it is running efficiently and achieving its aims.

FEEDBACK

For a team meeting system to work at its best, people must be confident that their concerns and questions reach the ears of the company's most senior managers. Formal feedback processes, with comments acknowledged or answered by senior managers, help create the feeling that involvement is worthwhile for all team members.

THE COMPANY'S SENIOR LINE MANAGER:

- reviews issues raised at team meetings and responds to concerns common to the unit as a whole;

●agrees which divisional messages are appropriate for the next round of team meetings.

THE SENIOR MANAGER RESPONSIBLE FOR COMMUNICATIONS:

●ensures that questions raised in team meetings and passed up the line are answered within a defined timescale;

●collates feedback on people's views and concerns raised in team meetings and feeds these back to the owners of the message;

●carries out a regular (usually annual) formal review of the team meeting system examining its structure, content and effectiveness, to ensure it does not fall into disrepute or disuse. This may be covered in local or national employee attitude research;

●maintains schedules of local team meetings and acts as the first point of reference on team meeting process-related questions for line managers;

●monitors the performance of local managers in running the meetings and assesses the need for further skills training.

SECOND LINE MANAGERS AND ABOVE:

●ensure that team meetings take place regularly and that team members understand the information that is put across;

●regularly attend team meetings throughout their unit to demonstrate their commitment to the system, and to support team leaders.

TEAM MEMBERS:

- attend meetings regularly;
- check that they understand messages briefed;
- express their views and concerns and ask questions.

WALKING THE JOB

Managers who are seen to be in touch are more effective. Regular contact between managers and their teams is as important to the success of every business as the contacts between the company and its customers and suppliers.

Walking the job or "management by walking about" is an opportunity for senior and line managers to build up this regular contact by setting aside time to visit the workplace to discuss, in an informal manner, individual and team achievements, ideas and problems.

As well as giving people at all levels of the organisation the opportunity to express their views directly to managers, walking the job enables managers to develop their leadership skills, demonstrate that they are all part of the company team and learn, at first hand, about the changing day-to-day operations for which they are responsible.

WHY WALK THE JOB?

Walking the job has benefits for both managers and their teams.

THE BENEFITS FOR MANAGERS INCLUDE:

- finding out what's going on: being directly in touch with their people and listening to the undistorted, first-hand views and concerns of those in the front line;

- knowing that their people will regard them as more interested, committed and approachable and will be more likely to accept and identify with what is required of them;

- experiencing the atmosphere in the workplace;

- the chance to get informal feedback from their people on issues already communicated formally through other channels;

- the opportunity to thank people personally for the work they have done;

- showing that they care about their people.

THE BENEFITS FOR TEAM MEMBERS INCLUDE:

- an opportunity to see and put their views to those in charge;

- an opportunity to hear what's going on "from the horse's mouth";

- a chance to say what they want from senior line managers;

- tangible evidence of management's real interest in and commitment to the people in the business and the problems they face in serving their customers;

- seeing their senior managers "live" the organisation's values.

Frequent walking the job quickly creates the expectation that managers will be seen in the workplace. In turn, once people are confident that their managers are not there to check up on them or catch them out, they will talk openly about their work. Such visits are an important way of establishing managers' credibility.

It is important to recognise that results will not be achieved instantly; walking the job is a process of building the trust that will allow people to talk openly. Once they are confident that the truth as they see it is taken seriously by those who can make a real difference, people will open up.

HOW TO WALK THE JOB

For many managers, walking the job may seem artificial and forced to begin with; they may feel a little uneasy about doing it themselves or about having more senior managers talking directly to their people. It is very important, therefore, to make sure that all managers understand the aims of walking the job and what is expected of them.

It is difficult to lay down hard and fast rules for such an essentially informal method of communication. However, there are a number of ingredients that will contribute to the success of walking the job: regularity, empathy between managers and their teams, sincerity and honesty. From these ingredients a number of simple do's and don'ts can be derived.

DO:

- set aside time for getting out into the workplace and turn up when you say you will;

- make clear your interests and reasons for being there;

- dress appropriately – you may be walking the job 'up a pole' or 'down a hole';

- plan to cover every area of responsibility within a defined period, particularly where your people's work involves external customers;

- find out in advance if there are any particular topics of interest or concern to the people you are going to see;

- ask local managers to introduce you to new team members;

- ensure that different team members are spoken to on each visit and that, over time, all team members are spoken to;

- ask questions primarily relating to the job and to customers;

- be positive and encouraging;

- use the person's first name;

- respond sympathetically to "whinges" but steer them back to the immediate supervisor/manager for action;

- have a disciplined routine for following up issues raised with you;

- hold routine meetings with your people at their workplace rather than in your office;

- speak your mind; your people expect your leadership;

- LISTEN!

- SMILE!

DON'T:

- always speak to the same people;

- answer questions on issues that should first have been raised through line managers;

- allow individuals to let off steam on potentially destructive issues;

- give an answer to a question if you are not sure that you are right or if you are breaching confidentiality;

- appear to be fault-spotting;

- single out trades union representatives for individual discussion on each visit;

- appear to be in a hurry to move on;

- raise your people's expectations unfairly or prematurely;

- criticise managers in the presence or hearing of the people who report to them;

- tell people what to do; your people do not expect you to replace their line managers, nor do they expect you always to have the answer at your fingertips;

- walk the job with a huge retinue.

MONITORING

Walking the job becomes really effective only when practised regularly by each manager and consistently across the unit.

Senior managers at all organisational levels should plan to see all their people face to face each year and should schedule a programme of workplace visits. Each manager should confirm that all his or her subordinate managers are walking the job and, on a regular basis, review with them their experience of doing so.

SUMMARY

Walking the job is a simple, often enjoyable and proven method of increasing and sustaining contacts between managers and their teams. It gives managers the opportunity to:

- find out what is going on in their teams;

- identify the problems and barriers that their people face;

- recognise the skills and achievements of people face to face;

- convey the values that are important to the business.

It also contributes to the successful teamwork that is so important to every company's future.

COMMUNICATING ORGANISATIONAL CHANGE

The environment in which most companies operate is changing faster than ever before. Advances in technology and new markets are generating opportunities – both at home and abroad – at an ever-increasing rate. At the same time, legislation and growing competition have increased the pressure on businesses to operate as cost-effectively as possible. As the world of business changes, so individual companies must change as well, to ensure that resources are used to the best possible advantage.

Such a volatile situation makes organisational change inevitable. Whether this involves setting up a new department, merging or expanding existing departments, relocation, redeployment or redundancy, the way in which it is communicated is vital. An ability to change in response to changing circumstances is a defining characteristic of successful companies.

There is a danger that organisational change will be seen as an annoying distraction at best and, at worst, as a source of confusion and insecurity. It is, therefore, essential that the reasons for and details of such change are communicated effectively. Line managers play the crucial role in this; they must be seen by their people to be acting, and not reacting, providing information, guidance and reassurance. This will help to:

- reinforce good management/employee relations;

- enhance involvement and encourage cooperation;

- sustain the quality of service offered to customers;

- minimise rumour, speculation and insecurity;

- maintain morale;

- achieve the change.

Given that change is part of business as usual, it needs to be managed and communicated as such.

TIMING

The timing and content of the first communication sets the tone for the whole exercise. When it becomes clear that organisational change will be required, the earliest possible announcement must be made even though much of the detail may not yet be available. If rumours are allowed to circulate before any announcement is made, managers will inevitably be forced onto the defensive. Once lost, the initiative is difficult to regain.

THE MESSAGE

The first message to employees should:

- announce what is planned and why;

- make clear the purpose of the new organisation and how it will contribute to the organisation's mission and vision;

- indicate the timescales involved;

- emphasise the opportunities arising from the change;

- indicate who is most likely to be affected and reassure them that they will get support and guidance during the period of transition;

- identify the people who are managing the change and those who will be able to provide relevant information;

- encourage people to ask questions of their line managers.

As matters develop, the guiding principles underlying all communications should be:

- tell the people affected as much as you can as early as possible;

- use the line managers to deliver messages whenever possible;

- respond to concerns raised; they can at least be acknowledged, if not answered fully;

- honour all commitments to communicate;

- do not communicate speculation.

COMMUNICATION CHANNELS

Decisions about how to deliver a message will depend upon the message itself and the audience it is aimed at. The following channels may all have a part to play:

- personal letter: from the owner of the change to everyone affected;

- team meetings: which may need to be more frequent than usual during the transitional period;

- formal management forums and informal employee forums;

- newsletters and bulletins;

- electronic mail: all users should have access to key information;

- profiles of new appointees: to make clear who "owns" the new organisation;

- organisation charts: to help individuals understand where they fit in;

- interim internal directories: to keep everyone in contact (when the new structure is in place a definitive directory should be issued);

- phone-based information lines: for putting across short items;

- videos and video conferencing: to ensure that everyone gets the same message (provided the scale of the change justifies the cost);

- a speak-up scheme: often a useful way of encouraging people to ask questions (anonymously if necessary) which they might not want to put directly to their managers;

●newspapers and magazines: useful for giving a more general view of the change and personal opinions.

COORDINATION OF COMMUNICATION

Employee communications professionals will be able to help you to define the key messages and advise you on which communication channels can best be used to reach particular target audiences. He or she should have sight of the information necessary to ensure that a consistent approach is adopted and that the right information is going to the right people at the right time.

The personnel manager will normally act as "change coordinator" for the unit. (Depending on the scale of the change and the number of people involved, it may be necessary to form a change coordination team.) He or she should be responsible for:

●arranging the distribution and updating of information;

●monitoring the effectiveness of the distribution process;

●identifying any problem areas and developing action plans;

●ensuring that line managers have sufficient information to enable them to answer their people's questions.

Employee communications managers will have a complementary role to play in coordinating the communication process.

MONITORING

Depending on the scale of the change, it is important to monitor the effectiveness of the various communications initiatives as they are delivered. This will help to tailor subsequent parts of the communications programme to meet the audience's real needs.

Additionally, once a major organisational change is complete, there should be an evaluation of the lessons learned. It might be worth considering how a questionnaire might help you to discover what people feel about their place in the new organisation and whether they felt that they were adequately communicated with while the changes were occurring.

By ensuring that they are visible and accessible, all managers have a role to play in the monitoring process.

CONCLUSION

Line managers are responsible for the effective communication of change to their people and every business relies on their being able to do so in a timely, efficient and effective way. The challenge is not just to minimise possible disruption but to ensure that an environment is created in which flexibility and the ability to change are seen as virtues and in which the benefits of the change are achieved.

SUCCESSFUL PRESENTATIONS

Presentation skills should be an essential part of any manager's repertoire. Good presentations convey the fact that the presenter cares and convince the individual members of the audience that their understanding and support are valued.

WHY GIVE A PRESENTATION?

Presentation skills complement other management communications techniques such as conducting team meetings and walking the job. They enable managers to get the same message, in a structured way, to a number of people, face to face. Subsequent question and answer sessions provide an opportunity to ensure that the message has got across. Presentations also have the advantages of boosting commitment, demonstrating leadership and identifying managers with the issues they present.

CODE OF PRACTICE

Successful presentations, whether to large audiences, in the boardroom or to smaller teams, conform to an elementary code of practice:

- establish clear objectives for the event and, if applicable, for each individual speaker;

- full rehearsals are essential not only for spotting gaps and overlaps but also for building confidence and helping to time the event. This rehearsal should, if possible, be held in the same place as the actual presentation to allow speakers to acclimatise.

- agree an allotted speaking time, taking account of the nature of the material and the target audience. DO NOT OVERRUN;

- if you are using a script, stick to it in order to avoid wrong-footing other speakers;

- never commit others to delivering anything not previously agreed;

- don't try to cram in too much information;

- don't use jargon or too many statistics;

- wherever appropriate, issue invitations that describe the event and state its objectives;

- turn up in good time before the audience is expected and make sure that everything works;

- tell the audience you will supply a copy of the slides and/or script. These should be handed out at the end of the event to prevent people reading when they should be listening to the speaker;

- use unifying themes to give your presentation identity – "Putting customers first", "Winning world markets", "Beating the competition" etc – but make sure that everyone understands them;

- DON'T SPEAK FOR MORE THAN 30 MINUTES!

- seek audience feedback – it makes members of the audience feel part of the event and helps to improve future events;

- after the event, review the extent to which these objectives were met, together with any feedback received. Identify aspects for improvement and record them for future use.

BALANCE

Successful presentations conform to the following pattern:

- **structure** – tell them what you are going to tell them; tell them why they should listen; preview the presentation and explain the domestic arrangements;

- **perspective** – tell them in a manner which relates to their situation, concerns and experience;

- **elaboration** – enliven the presentation with analogies, meaningful examples, references to research etc. When recognising success and thanking people, name them;

- **emphasis** – tell them what you have just told them; restate its importance; thank them for listening; invite questions; tell them how you will deal with feedback.

TECHNIQUE

Public speaking is a skill that can be learned and is worth working on. Many training providers offer presentation skills courses to meet most managers' needs; many companies offer more advanced training and there are also publications offering useful tips.

When giving a presentation you should pay close attention to:

- **your voice** – speak clearly, audibly and not too fast, taking care to modulate your voice as appropriate and make good use of pauses;

- **your lines of sight** – make sure that you can see everyone and look regularly at all sections of the audience, not at your presentation aids;

- **your mannerisms** – avoid theatricals, fiddling with watches and pens etc because this is always distracting.

However, be yourself – it won't work otherwise.

QUESTION AND ANSWER SESSIONS

There are various approaches. For example, it should be possible with a smallish audience to answer questions directly from the floor. With larger audiences it will probably be necessary to give them a chance to submit questions in writing in advance.

Defensive, accusatory or long-winded answers inhibit potential questioners, while answering a question with a question tends to have a negative effect. In general, discussions need to be controlled if everyone is to have a chance to participate and certain subjects are to be prevented from dominating the agenda. Displaying the ground rules on a screen during the discussion can help.

Openness and trust are fostered by allowing questioners the right of reply to the answer given or at least by checking that the answer really addresses the question asked.

It is important to be seen to answer all questions and not just those that are easy or politically acceptable. If you genuinely do not know the answer say so immediately, agree some way of following the issue up with the questioner and follow it up. Never try to disguise your lack of knowledge by answering an unasked question instead.

SLIDES

Effective slides, whether OHPs or 35mm, are an integral feature of successful presentations. However, avoid the temptation to introduce too many – a maximum of one for every three minutes of the presentation is sufficient. Other rules of thumb are:

- be clear and concise and don't use more than 25 words per slide (the "five by five" rule);

- diagrams should be as simple as possible;

- don't mix typefaces or use fancy effects like shadowed text;

- don't include too many numbers;

- make sure your slides properly reflect your company's image or identity if presenting to an external or public audience;

- in the case of OHP slides, use black on clear for the most part and always avoid pale colours in diagrams;

- for 35mm slides use white or light text on a dark background.

CONCLUSION

Presentations offer managers opportunities to set messages in the context of main business activities. On occasions there will be "hard" messages to deliver calling for dramatic improvements; at other times the message will be "more of the same winning formula"; but whatever the event, there is always the opportunity to thank people publicly for their efforts, to inspire and motivate them and to enhance team spirit.

COMMUNICATING FINANCIAL PERFORMANCE

A company's financial results are the key indicator of how that company is performing and of its future prospects. The announcement of financial results is often accompanied by comment in the media and elsewhere, much of it unfavourable.

In financial matters, as in so much else, it is hard to please all of the people all of the time. Indeed it is quite possible to be castigated at one and the same time for delivering high profits (by the press), for failing to do so (by shareholders), for doing so but reducing employee numbers (by trades unions), or for doing so but failing to reduce numbers quickly enough (by City analysts). It is, therefore, extremely important that people understand not just the figures and what they mean, but are also aware that individual contributions and cost–consciousness make all the difference.

This may be difficult sometimes because financial matters tend to be seen as the property of accountants who speak their own private language and the amounts of money involved can be so large it is difficult for individuals to relate them to everyday experience. Given this, it is vital when communicating financial results at any level to ask: "What do these results mean to this audience? What messages must I get across and in what ways should these results prompt our people to act differently in the future?"

As well as communicating financial information, we need to communicate financial messages. Straightforward reporting of company performance must be supplemented by a shared understanding of the importance of profit optimisation and cost control, as they apply to day-to-day operations, and the key relationship between profits, prices and investment. At the same time, we must build an awareness of the impact of competition, of regulation and of our customers' perception of the value for money we offer.

COMPANY RESULTS

Company results are usually issued each quarter and published externally with an accompanying press release. At the end of the financial year, full year results are also published in outline in an Annual Report and commented on in an Annual Review, both of which are available to all shareholders. For legal reasons results cannot be revealed to employees before they are issued to the public. The aim is therefore for simultaneous publication, internally and externally.

The quarterly results and associated press release should be immediately copied to every employee communications manager, as soon as they are available, enabling them to package and present the material in a suitable format for their audience. Quarter by quarter, this will build understanding and accustom managers to receiving and briefing this kind of information.

MAKING RESULTS MEANINGFUL

It is vital to give meaning to the large numbers in reports and draw out their relevance for the company as a whole, the unit or division, teams and individuals.

One way of doing this is to identify and explain the main financial measures – turnover, investment, pre-tax and post-tax profits – compare them with previous performance and draw clear conclusions. In this context, people should understand that the media concentrate primarily on pre-tax profits and that this is by no means the end of the story. Taxation, for instance, takes about one third of pre-tax profits away. Then there are the dividends to be paid to shareholders and a significant proportion of the costs of capital expenditure and investment programme to be met. By the time all these essential deductions have been made, the initial pre-tax profit may even have been reduced to a cash deficit.

PROFITS IN PERSPECTIVE

People clearly have difficulty reconciling external comment about "huge profits" and internal messages about keeping costs down and seeking value for money. Only by acknowledging, summarising and commenting on the external reaction to the results, and putting claims of "£X per second profit" in the perspective of what it has to pay for, can this difficulty be resolved. In fact, of course, this apparent "clash" of messages is largely manufactured by external commentators.

BUDGET MANAGEMENT

It is important to get across the message that good performance against budget is the key measure of success. This is not a miraculous but a managed process – managers must set out clearly their team's objectives and the process for achieving them, and so build an awareness of the importance of financial management among team members.

When preparing a budget, managers must demonstrate to their team that the planned expenditure is realistic and achievable and that it is based on a clear understanding of business needs and priorities. Clarity at an early stage helps to avoid difficulties later in the year.

IMPACT ON PLANS

It is also essential that people recognise that in an increasingly competitive environment it is sometimes necessary to adjust current budgets and plans, while remaining committed to overall strategies and aims. A company's ability to invest depends on raising the necessary income and if performance drops, it is inevitable that the organisation must cut its cloth accordingly. Companies must continually look at ways of increasing income and reducing failure costs, in order to minimise the risk to plans.

UNIT RESULTS

Company results are, of course, ultimately based on the sum total of a multitude of local performances and are, therefore, only part of the story. Each unit (division, directorate, section, group, team) must review its own financial performance on a monthly basis, using information from the various financial monitoring systems. This can best be done in team meetings where the team leader has an opportunity to discuss team performance face to face with the team members and check that they understand the meaning of the results. Every team member needs to know how the team is performing, what changes need to be made and what his or her personal role is to be.

In team meetings, begin by looking at variances (under/overspends) on budget – capital, non-pay, pay, staff, internal transfer charge. The team must understand that a single wayward month can have serious implications for the full year's performance. The team is then responsible for identifying and implementing appropriate remedial action; whenever possible, specific actions should be allocated to individual team members.

SUMMARY

There is clear evidence from attitude research that people want to understand how their company is performing financially, what impact the competition is having and how their own efforts in seeking greater value for money contribute to company success. The effective communication of financial performance and of the business environment in which that performance is achieved can deliver this perspective regularly and in a most emphatic way.

It is not simply a question of ensuring that people have the relevant numbers, but of ensuring that they understand what those numbers mean to them as individuals, to their work group and to the company as a whole. Clear explanation leads to understanding, clear understanding leads to commitment and commitment leads to improved performance.

COMMUNICATING ATTITUDE SURVEY RESULTS

Regular surveys of employees' views on a wide range of subjects, including their jobs, terms and conditions, training and appraisals, their managers, their customers, employee communications and the company as a whole have become a common feature in many companies.

Results can show not only what people's attitudes and opinions are at the time of the survey but also how these attitudes and opinions are changing over time. These results can be a major input to the business planning process.

BRINGING THE RESULTS TO LIFE

Just like customer satisfaction measures, financial results and quality of service figures, the results of employee attitude surveys provide vital information about how the company is performing and whether or not it is meeting its targets.

The communications challenge is the same in all these cases: how can managers make all this information and all these numbers interesting and meaningful to their individual teams? Only if they can do so will their teams fully understand and own any action plans formulated in response to these results.

Whatever the size of the group to which you are presenting the results, the underlying principle remains the same: results are produced, interpreted and communicated not for their own sake but as a trigger for action. The question to keep always in mind is: "How can we use these results to improve the way we all work to achieve the company's aims?"

WHY COMMUNICATE?

Apart from the general need to maintain a successful manager/employee dialogue – keeping your people up to date with developments that affect them and giving them the opportunity to air their views – there are a number of particular reasons for keeping them in touch with attitude survey results:

- you have the chance to interpret the results for your people and discuss with them what action should be taken within your team;

- your people can see that the survey gives them a chance to communicate their views upwards and that their views are valued and will be acted on whenever possible;

- you can increase your people's identification with and understanding of the survey process, so increasing the chances that they will fill in and return any questionnaires that they are sent in the future.

WHAT TO COMMUNICATE?

The following are some guidelines to some of the essential areas:

- Key results: general issues eg. pride in the company;

- changes year-on-year: better/worse;

- trends: changes over a longer period of time;

- comparison: between the teams, business units and the company's overall results.

HOW TO COMMUNICATE

Face-to-face, two-way methods should form the main part of any communication of the results but this does not mean that other methods cannot be used. Articles in company publications, letters and other written communications will also be used to put the message across. Employee communications managers will be able to advise about what coverage is planned in your business unit.

Using face-to-face methods such as team meetings means that:

- you can thank your people personally for taking part in the survey;

- you can ask for suggestions about how to achieve any necessary improvements;

- you can demonstrate your willingness to listen and respond to any concerns they may have about the results and their implications;

- you can check your people's understanding of the results and their implications;

- you can ensure that the views of your people are communicated upwards.

YOUR PEOPLE'S VIEWS

One way of giving additional relevance is to ask your people the following questions about each of the results you have identified as being significant for the unit as a whole:

- do they feel that the results nationally and/or for their business unit are a fair reflection of their own views? (It is important that they understand that even if they do not believe that their views are reflected, this does not invalidate the data collected.)

- why do they think people might have answered in that way?

- what problems or shortcomings, if any, does the result suggest?

- what can they do, together, to bring about any improvements? (Action must, of course, be coordinated across and between units in order to avoid duplication of effort.)

- what should you do to facilitate their bringing about these improvements?

BALANCE AND TIMING

All communications must be balanced and timely. Concentrating solely on the positive or negative results, or attempting to explain away inconvenient ones, will alienate your audience. They will know that both good and bad things are bound to emerge from any survey and they will not be interested in, nor find it easy to relate to, messages that seem to them to be biased in either direction.

It is very important to communicate results as quickly as possible. This will help to demonstrate your interest in, and openness about, the survey and its results. It will also make it easier to draw out the relevance of the results for your audience. People's opinions change, so a long delay between questionnaires being filled in and the results being communicated can make the messages seem like "ancient history".

CONCLUSION

Attitude survey results are a valuable business resource. They provide a statistically valid and widely accepted basis for future planning and action. For this to happen, the results must be interpreted intelligently and communicated in a way that brings out their relevance for the audience.

LEADING YOUR TEAM

At times of unsettling change, leaders are the people who thrive on that change, who manage it, and are seen to manage it, in a quality way. Good communication skills are fundamental to good leadership.

In one sense, leaders are simply the people who personify the recommendations in this booklet: they build trust amongst their people, run effective team meetings, regularly walk the job, are accomplished presenters and have the ability to make all kinds of business information interesting and relevant to their people.

The ability to inspire and involve is the other key attribute. People are a leader's most important resource. Leaders enlist the active participation of their teams, making full use of all their talents and capacity for innovation. However, a good leader not only gets the most out of his or her people, but also ensures that they, in their turn, get the most out of what they do in terms of job satisfaction and the reward and recognition they deserve.

Leaders are proud of the company they work for, are enthusiastic about what it does and communicate that enthusiasm to their teams and their customers alike.

MANAGING CHANGE

Of course, leaders do not achieve major change themselves; their teams do that. Leaders make this possible by:

- stating and explaining the company's mission, vision and values and demonstrating the key link between these and day-to-day operations;

- establishing clear priorities and standards;

- setting demanding but achievable targets;

- explaining why key decisions have been taken;

- as far as possible, involving all team members in all team activities and getting the best out of everybody;

- encouraging innovation and demonstrating a willingness to experiment with new ideas and new ways of doing things (whilst, at the same time, minimising the risk to standards of service);

- ensuring that the resources necessary to do the job – people, money, time etc – are available;

- recognising, reinforcing and rewarding the desired behaviour in team members;

- communicating progress towards objectives (even if this sometimes means communicating lack of progress);

- keeping a sense of perspective; relating short-term tasks to longer-term objectives;

- minimising disagreement;

- evaluating results and comparing them with the original objectives;

- LISTENING!

INNOVATION

Good leaders encourage innovation by:

- recognising that a listening style of leadership is essential;

- welcoming ideas and innovations which originate from further down or elsewhere in the organisation;

- delegating whenever appropriate and not getting hung up on detail;

- allowing their people the freedom, where appropriate, to approach others further up or elsewhere in the organisation with ideas and suggestions;

- praising new ideas (not just thinking of reasons not to do something) and suggesting how they might be implemented;

- treating problems as opportunities for improvement rather than as a sign of weakness or failure;

- remembering that they do not have all the answers.

TRUST

Leaders have to earn the trust of the people they lead. Trust is what holds teams together – without it, nothing happens. You cannot hope to win the trust of your people if they perceive a gap between what you say and what you do. Whether the issue is cost-consciousness or living by the company's values, leading can only be done from the front and by example.

You don't need genius or educational qualifications to win the trust of your people – many leaders manage perfectly well without conspicuous charisma. Consistency is what really matters, demonstrating that you mean what you say and that it applies to you as much as to everyone else, and taking responsibility for the team's mistakes as well as its successes.

DEVELOPING PEOPLE

One effective way in which to win that trust is to take an active part in the individual development of the members of your team, and to ensure that they:

- know what they have to do to make a difference;

- feel that the job is challenging and that they have a level of responsibility that matches their abilities;

- have control over those aspects of the job for which they are accountable;

- receive regular feedback on their performance and coaching to improve any areas of weakness.

MEASURING SUCCESS

Attitude surveys provide an opportunity to measure the extent to which managers have been effective leaders, how well they have communicated and gained acceptance of the company's vision and whether or not their people understand how their activities contribute to the wider company goals. They can also provide information about the degree to which people are given help when necessary, consulted about decisions, given the opportunity to become involved in quality improvements and have a good sense of teamwork.

WRITTEN COMMUNICATIONS

However important your subject, however committed you are to communicating it widely, if you don't express yourself clearly it is unlikely that you will get your message across. The way you write it is one of the things that will determine whether or not what you say will be acted on.

Writing good, unambiguous prose does not come naturally to everyone; but it can be worked at. There are a number of useful guides, including:

- George Orwell, "Politics and the English Language", in *Inside the Whale and other Essays* (Penguin);

- Keith Waterhouse, *Waterhouse on Newspaper Style* (Viking);

- Sir Ernest Gowers, *Complete Plain Words* (HMSO).

APPROACH

Every time you have something to write, no matter whether it is an office memo or a report for the chairman, ask yourself the following questions:

- who am I writing this for and how much do they already know about the subject? Make sure that you provide all the necessary background, but don't bore your readers with unnecessary historical information;

- what length, style and layout will suit the reader?

- what do I want to say and what do I want the reader to do once I have said it?

- what will the structure be? Recommendation: a brief introduction explaining why the reader should read it; the message itself; a clear conclusion;

- what are the best words to use?

- could I have been briefer?

Once you have produced a first draft, try reading it aloud or, better still, ask a colleague to read it for you.

ORWELL'S RULES

More than 40 years ago, George Orwell formulated a number of rules for the writing of effective English; these are as useful today as when they were written. Orwell's rules can be summarised as:

- never use an image or a figure of speech which you have seen many times before ("avoid clichés like the plague");

- never use a long word if a shorter word can do the same job (the term for using long words instead of short ones is "sesquipedalianism");

- if it is possible to cut out a word or phrase or sentence or paragraph without the meaning suffering – cut it (when in doubt, leave it out);

- never use passives if you can use actives (always say "I decided" rather than "it was decided");

- never use jargon if there is an everyday English equivalent.

Follow these rules, and you will produce clear, functional prose. Orwell, however, added one more:

- break all the above rules rather than write anything that you know to be ugly or "barbarous".

OTHER RULES

One could include as many rules as space permits, but the following are some of the more important:

- don't use too many abstract nouns;

- don't split infinitives – in spite of *Star Trek*, "to go boldly" is correct and "to boldly go" is not;

- don't mix metaphors – what would happen if you buried an old chestnut or nipped a red herring in the bud?

- don't be afraid of full stops – overlong sentences can be confusing;

- don't use too many subordinate clauses in a single sentence;

- never be "ongoing" – the word "ongoing" rarely adds anything, try "continuing";

- make sure that your tenses are consistent and that your pronouns agree with their nouns;

- be careful about singulars and plurals – for example "the Board" and "the Company" are both singular.

WORDS AND MEANINGS

Words and phrases do not exist in isolation, nor are they neutral. The way we write about things can be an excuse for not really thinking about them or can betray our attitudes towards them. The difference between "subscribers" and "customers", "staff" and "people" is enormous and not just linguistic. On the other hand, the uncritical repetition of phrases like "our company values its people", "satisfied customers", "adding value", "year on year improvements", "culture change" and so on can deprive them of any meaning. Such phrases are useful only if used sparingly. Moral: you are the one saying it; pick your words carefully.

THE WAFFLE FACTOR

There is a tendency for written English to be padded out with meaningless phrases. People are much more likely to write than to say things like: "not unrelated to", "at this moment in time", "a means of adding value to", "the question as to whether", "greatly to be desired", "in terms of", "by means of" and so on. Don't be fooled, however, waffle may sound posher and more official but it has the major drawbacks of conveying almost no information and being instantly forgettable. All such phrases can safely be abandoned – no one will regret their passing.

ABBREVIATIONS

The use of abbreviations is endemic. Customers and employees alike are required to make sense of such sentences as "I've spoken to DCR about the SLA between PSM ECMs and the CCU." Three letter abbreviations (TLA) can spread like a virus through all parts of an organisation. Convenient though they are as a shorthand, there is a danger that they will obscure your meaning.

The rules are:

- only use abbreviations if writing the phrase in full would be cumbersome or pedantic;

- if you must use an abbreviation, give the phrase in full (with the abbreviation in brackets afterwards) the first time you use it, but from then on only use the abbreviation;

- don't, whatever you do, invent any more abbreviations.

QUANTITY AS WELL AS QUALITY

You should, of course, continually monitor the amount as well as the quality of the paperwork that you produce. Too much non-essential information circulates in most companies; so, whenever you are thinking of adding to the paper that crosses people's desks, consider:

- is it necessary to write at all? Wouldn't a quick call achieve as much in a fraction of the time and at far less cost?

- must this communication go to everyone or could it be more precisely targeted?

- do people really need copies for information if no action is required of them?

- is daily/weekly/monthly distribution really necessary?

- is there scope for bundling similar items into bulletins?

CONCLUSION

A clear prose style is an essential part of every manager's repertoire; a well-turned sentence can be as valuable as a well-run meeting or a satisfied customer.

EFFECTIVE LISTENING

The main problem with listening is that we don't usually recognise that it requires conscious effort. After all, we do it all the time. There is a tendency to assume that the responsibility for the success or failure of communication rests with the speaker, whereas, in fact, the listener has an equally important part to play. Listening is an active not a passive process, something that can be done well or badly, and is a fundamental part of every manager's repertoire of communications skills.

Of the four basic communications skills – listening, speaking, reading and writing – listening is the one that receives the least formal attention and yet, like the others, it is a skill that can be learned. We also spend a lot more time listening than we do reading or writing. It has been estimated that as much as 60 per cent of our working lives is spent listening – an important reason for getting it right. Effective listening saves time, cuts down on (costly) misunderstanding, is essential to good teamwork and provides one of the best opportunities for showing that we respect other people's views.

We listen for many different reasons: to be polite, to get some precise information, to understand a problem, to sympathise, to find fault and so on. How we listen will depend on why we are listening and what we are listening for. If we are aware of these things, we are likely to listen more effectively.

BARRIERS TO EFFECTIVE LISTENING

There are many reasons why we do not always listen as well and carefully as we should:

- we get too emotionally involved in the issues and hear only what we want to hear (or fail to hear what we do not wish to hear);

- we allow personal feelings about the speaker to prejudice our judgment of what he or she has to say (try to listen to the speech rather than the speaker);

- we are too impatient, too eager to take over the talking;

- we may be thinking about something else and not giving the issue in question our full attention;

- we are distracted by the appearance, mannerisms or style of the speaker;

- we are too ready to think about other things, to treat our turn to listen as an excuse for a rest.

All these barriers can be demolished but only if we devote the same care and attention to listening as we do to speaking or writing. Awareness of the barriers is the first step towards improving performance; every company needs a communications culture in which managers pride themselves on being good listeners.

Of course, there are other problems which often are the fault of the speaker – too much information, delivery too rapid and so on – but by making the speaker aware of these (without appearing too critical) the issue can often be resolved. (For more on this see page 21 – *Successful presentations*.)

BEING A GOOD LISTENER

So, what are the characteristics of a good listener? A good listener:

- always knows what he or she wishes to achieve from a dialogue;

- always develops a strategy for achieving it;

- always prepares by doing the background reading and having a clear view of the purpose of the exchange;

- gives advance consideration to the kinds of questions that will be appropriate, how to put them sensitively and how to gauge reaction;

- allows the speaker to finish without interrupting and without finishing sentences on the speaker's behalf;

- maintains eye contact;

- avoids inappropriate body language (yawning, looking out of the window, falling asleep etc);

- avoids leading or deliberately embarrassing questions;

- remembers that dialogue is not about winning and losing but achieving a shared understanding;

- uses questions to create further listening opportunities;

- confirms his or her understanding with the speaker;

- generally does whatever is necessary to maximise the value of the dialogue.

BEING SEEN TO LISTEN

It is not enough simply to listen well – it is essential to be seen (by the speaker) to listen well. There is nothing worse than talking to an expressionless, silent listener. Speakers need to be reassured that they are making sense and to be encouraged to give of their best. Non-verbal communication is critical here. Think about the effect that a yawn at the wrong time might have!

You are the lucky owner of a sophisticated range of facial expressions, gestures, postures and so on which can make life easier for the speaker and the exchange more profitable for both of you.

MAKING THE MOST OF SPARE CAPACITY

It has been calculated that people talk at about 120/150 words per minute, are capable of hearing and making sense of at least 400 words per minute, and can think at 800 words per minute. This means that listeners have in some sense to "slow down" to keep pace with the speaker, which can adversely affect concentration.

Such spare capacity can be used constructively. Listening is an active process which involves continuously monitoring what is being said, analysing its relevance, its connections with things you already know and the action likely to be required of you. If you can do all this, many workplace conversations are likely to seem a lot less dull!

CONSCIOUS HEARING

Effective listening has been defined as "conscious hearing". The value of such a definition is that it stresses the importance of consciously polishing up an essentially unconscious act. By becoming conscious of the ways we listen and respond, we are likely to improve the way we do both.

The importance of an open mind cannot be overstated; there are a number of valid views of the world. Listening carefully to someone does not imply that you agree with what they say and, in any case, you are not always required to judge whether or not what they are saying is correct.

Even in an adversarial situation you will do best to listen carefully to what the other person has to say; you can then focus debate on what you regard as the weak points of their position.

Remember: an argument, no matter how vigorous or therapeutic, no matter how much fun, may be little more than a failure to communicate.

COMMUNICATING BAD NEWS

If the news was always good, there would be no particular need for managers to develop interpersonal and communications skills. However badly you put it, the news that someone is going to receive an enormous bonus is likely to find favour with that person. Similarly, there would be little difficulty in persuading employees (if not shareholders) to support the proposition that the company should triple their annual holiday.

LIFE ISN'T LIKE THAT

Unfortunately, life was never like that, and is getting less so. Given the growth of competition and the need to balance the requirements of investors, customers, employees and legislation, the news is often uncomfortable and can be downright painful. Managers are increasingly required to be the bearers of tidings that will not always find favour with their people: the company is having to rebalance its workforce; the department is closing/shrinking/relocating etc.

The Ancient Greeks had a simple way of dealing with bad news, they killed the messenger who brought it. If only to avoid a similar fate, managers need to be sensitive to the impact on their audience of unwelcome news and deal with it constructively. It would be naive, for example, to expect people to respond with delight to the news that their services are no longer required. Equally, delivering bad news is itself a painful process. However, it certainly is possible to handle the communication in such a way as (at the very least) to make the best of a difficult job so that people can go with dignity and without bitterness or a sense of having been unfairly treated.

Textbooks on communications theory have little to say on the subject, preferring a conflictless view of management. On such an analysis, information is an essentially neutral commodity and the job of communications is simply ensuring that the right bits of it get to the right people in the right place at the right time and in the appropriate format.

This view fails to take account of the fact that some information will never be palatable, no matter how professionally packaged.

A FEW GENERAL PRINCIPLES

There are general principles which may help managers to handle such situations more effectively:

- the golden rule is that if the news is bad, never try to pretend that it is good. To be expected to find consolation in the fact that although one is being made redundant, at least no one else in the team is, requires a good deal more altruism than the average human can muster;

- try to understand, both emotionally and intellectually, what your message means to those on the receiving end. Before you undertake the communication, find out what you can about your audience – what are they expecting, what do they know already, what are their aspirations, what has their recent performance been etc?

- people's reactions will vary, but may include fear, anger, frustration and self-doubt. If people are upset, there is no benefit in pretending that they are not or suggesting that their response is irrational. You will need to acknowledge the fact and help them to understand and find ways of dealing with their own feelings. Show your concern;

- remember that the way you communicate the news will provide a role model for the way in which your audience responds;

- when communicating bad news it is even more important than usual to make sure that you listen to the response and deal with it sympathetically. People who have just had bad news are probably entitled to express their feelings before bowing to the inevitable;

- when delivering bad news, get it right. You have an extra responsibility to ensure that your message is sufficiently researched, clearly expressed and appropriately packaged, contains all the necessary information and makes plain what the options are. You might be forgiven for making a hash of good news but not for delivering confused bad news;

- stick to the facts; bad news is unlikely to be made any more palatable by your commenting (either positively or negatively) on it;

- resist the temptation to pass the buck. It is no good blaming "them up there". You may not be responsible for the decisions but encouraging dissent (and risking non-compliance) is unprofessional;

- bad news can only be communicated successfully in an atmosphere of mutual trust. This is not something over which you have absolute control – mistrust may have been building up for years before you arrived – and you cannot reverse this trend at a moment's notice. It is important, therefore, that every communication with your people should be honest and straightforward;

- find out what specialist support is available (from your personnel unit, employee communications manager etc) and don't be afraid to ask for help;

- it is a good idea to rehearse the communications exercise beforehand, perhaps with the help of an experienced counsellor or facilitator.

CASE STUDIES

Of course, there is no such thing as employee communications by numbers, but the following two case studies might suggest some ways in which difficult situations can be made "less worse" than they might otherwise have been.

You have to ask for volunteers to leave the company on an early release scheme.

- remember at all times that the news you are delivering has the power, quite literally, to change people's lives;

- resist the temptation to hand it over to specialists. Your people have a right to hear the bad news from you and are more likely to respond positively if it comes from you;

- unless the bad news affects the entire team, break it first to those affected, face to face and in private. Allow them sufficient time to react – don't rush it simply because it's unpleasant;

- although you will need to say something about the strategic reasons for reducing numbers, and put your local reduction in the context of the company's objectives as a whole, do not make too much of this;

- help your people to understand their options. Information about pensions, redundancy payments etc should be presented with a certain formality;

- don't be too ready with glib remarks about how you wish you were in their place and how lucky they are to be able to make a fresh start. This may not be how they see it;

- make sure that people know where to go for further information;

- make yourself available for further discussions.

You have to "sell" a 20 per cent budget cut to your team.

- make clear from the start that you intend to implement the change;

- point out that budget cuts are not value judgments or punishment for bad behaviour. They are often a response to a change in economic circumstances affecting the company as a whole;

- make it clear to your team that you can only deliver what the company requires with their help;

- such a message cannot really be made sense of unless it is related to the company's overall business plans and perhaps to the condition of the economy as a whole;

- the connection between local cost savings (which may be small) and overall savings (which may be huge) must be clearly stated;

- avoid fruitless discussion about whether or not the cuts should be made but seek advice on where such cuts should be made with the least detrimental impact on the team's work;

- do not dissociate yourself from the decision and, as far as possible, emphasise the need in all successful businesses for cost control and good housekeeping;

- once the cut has been achieved, do not forget that it ever happened, but monitor its impact on team performance.

CONCLUSION

"Macho" management – "here's the bad news, like it or lump it" – has no place in a mature company. Managers cannot ensure that the news they have to give is always good, but they can ensure that the news is communicated professionally and sensitively. Truisms about valuing people are just that, unless we can underpin them with behaviour that shows we really do care.

As for the vexed question of how we can communicate bad news better, it is important to remember that it is a two-way process. At times of change, your people need to be persuaded that they should speak up and that nothing is to be gained by remaining silent. You have a responsibility to feed back up the line your people's responses and your own suggestions as to how things could be improved next time.

SAYING THANK YOU

When was the last time you thanked one of your people for a job well done? When was the last time the efforts you make in your job were acknowledged by your line manager?

Sometimes managers are so busy dealing with day-to-day business and the occasional crisis that they don't have time to recognise particular successes or improvements in performance within their own teams. Others even question the need to thank people "just for doing their jobs".

But if managers are accountable when things go wrong, we are equally responsible for behaving professionally when things go well: managers deliver results only through their teams, and improving and maintaining team performance is the fundamental purpose of a manager's job.

The issue becomes then, how do we support positive actions with positive feedback? Saying thank you makes the difference and is clearly an integral part of every manager's job.

FEELING VALUED

We all know that everyone needs to feel valued in order to give of their best and many commentators consider that being recognised for one's achievements is the most powerful motivator there can be. From the recipient's perspective you can never say thank you too often.

Recognition for good work – for living by company values – cannot simply be left to a formal awards scheme. It must become common practice among good managers.

Saying thank you shows people what is expected, what can be done and helps to create a supportive working environment where people know their best efforts will be recognised.

OPPORTUNITIES TO SAY THANK YOU

Managers should thank their people whenever anything goes well, and particularly:

- to encourage or reinforce the kinds of behaviour that the company needs to continue to be successful;

- whenever a team member or the team as a whole hits or exceeds a set target;

- when meeting customer needs requires work above and beyond the normal call of duty;

- when a team member or the team as a whole has made a special effort and you want to encourage them to sustain, maintain and/or repeat that effort in future;

- to show the company's and your own appreciation of effective performance or of delivering measurable improvements to the way you do things.

Remember: failure to recognise when someone has done well can, conversely, be one of the most demoralising and demotivating of work experiences.

HOW DO I SAY THANK YOU?

There can be no hard and fast rules, nor is there a single approach that will necessarily suit all managers. You will need to feel comfortable with whatever approach you choose to take. However, there are a number of general principles you can follow to help make saying thank you less of a formal and stilted process.

- **be natural** – everyone has their own style. Relax. Your people will listen happily as long as you are clear, open and honest when giving your thanks;

- **be on time** – don't put it off or leave saying thank you to a special event. Recognise people's contributions throughout the year and as near as possible to the time the particular effort was made. The closer the link between behaviour and thanks, the easier it is for others to learn the lessons;

- **be specific** – avoid being too general with your thanks. Be factual and make sure people understand exactly why they are being thanked and what criteria you have used to judge any award they are to be offered;

- **be appropriate** – don't go "over the top" unless you really believe the behaviour warrants such praise. Try to ensure that the level of your appreciation matches the value of the work done; use the full range of options open to you to recognise achievement;

- **be open** – don't be shy about recognising success and don't be "backward at coming forwards" – take pride in your team's achievements. Team members' pride in their own work and achievements – and, by implication, their future performance – can be raised significantly by publicly thanking them for what they have done, whether at a team meeting or other formal or informal get-togethers. Other managers and their teams also need to know about your successes if, as a company, you are to share best practice efficiently. Remember that recognition loses much of its power if it is not made public;

- **emphasise the success** – describe the improved performance, its relevance to the team, to other teams and its potential effect on the wider company. If the behaviour or action has definable impact on financial or quality of service measures, be explicit about how and where the effects will show up and how they will ultimately contribute;

●**be straightforward** – don't tarnish the praise by using the opportunity to tackle other problems or to gain agreement to other commitments. All the advantages of saying thank you will be dissipated if your people think you are using it merely to soften them up for bad news or more hard work.

You can say thank you at any time, but your choice will determine how important the rest of the team perceive the event (and the thanks) to be.

Whether you say thank you in public or privately, whilst walking the job during the normal working day or at a team meeting, you will inevitably be providing a role model for the team. Thanks can also be reinforced at appraisal times and during performance reviews.

DOING THE RIGHT THING

There are many ways to show your appreciation for a job well done, ranging from a simple, spoken "thank you" to a letter of thanks; from a bonus recommendation to a formal award under a recognition scheme. The choice is yours but you will need to be sure that, if more than a simple thank you is needed, the reward matches the level of effort or improvement made.

There are many ways you can publicise your team's successes – at a local level you can use noticeboards, team meetings, employee evenings and/or newsletters. On a broader front, company publications are always keen to cover successes in both local and national pages. Contact your employee communications manager if you need further help or advice.

Some companies have a formal framework for recognition. Line managers should take the lead role in making the recognition scheme work by recognising behaviour which supports company values among members of their own team, by nominating people in other teams for the good work they do and by making awards and saying thank you to their own team, following customer or other nominations. Notable local successes may be considered for further awards at zone, function, directorate, divisional or even national levels, leading in some cases to annual Awards for Quality.

Saying *'thank you'* is all about encouraging people to live by the company values. To survive in an increasingly competitive world, your company must be the sort which instinctively puts its customers first; which acts professionally; and which strives always to improve the way you do things for the benefit of your customers. As managers, the trick is to make this happen in your own teams. Saying *'thank you'* can be a powerful first step. Don't underestimate it!

UPWARD COMMUNICATION

It is increasingly important for the people who actually do the work or meet the customers to be able to communicate swiftly and effectively with decision-makers.

Where there is a problem with products or service delivery which affects the quality of goods or services, the people at the front line of the organisation are usually the first to know. It can often take time for the reaction from customers to filter back to the senior management of the organisation. Sometimes the customers never do feed back the problem, waste or inefficiency continue, and the business loses customers. An organisation which can free the channels of communication between the front line people and decision-makers has a real competitive advantage over others.

Some organisations relish customer complaints as they can help pinpoint ways of improving goods or services. In the same way, organisations are now realising that the problems and concerns that their employees identify, especially at the front edge, give them the opportunity for continuous improvement.

There are three sorts of issues that need to be communicated from the people at the front edge of the organisation:

- **problems** and other issues preventing them from doing their job as well as they otherwise might;

- **ideas** they may have arising from their greater knowledge of the work and of their particular customers, internal or external;

- **views and concerns** of those likely to be affected, before a decision is made. Their knowledge can contribute to making a better decision and they are more likely to be committed to implementing a change when they have been involved in designing it.

There may be channels of communication in the organisation which encourage "upward" communication, such as "Speak Up" systems or an internal complaints procedure. Whether or not such channels exist, managers have a major role to play in encouraging open communication within their teams and in solving or passing on information about problems.

ENCOURAGING UPWARD COMMUNICATION

The first prerequisite for successful upward communication is successful downward communications. Unless people understand the aims of the job in the wider context of the organisation's aims and priorities, they are unlikely to be able to see the problems they face in perspective. So a manager needs to make sure that employees are well informed about organisational issues by making sure that they:

- attend team meetings and that these meetings include information about the wider organisation as well as about performance matters;

- have the opportunity and are encouraged to attend larger meetings held by senior managers such as roadshows, annual presentations etc;

- receive the various publications the organisation produces about its progress and aims, and are encouraged to read them;

- attend an induction programme when they first join the organisation.

USING THE SYSTEM

Where there are systems for upward communication in the organisation, you can encourage people to use them:

- by making sure that they know the systems exist;

- by suggesting that they use the channels when they raise matters informally and by publicly praising any successes achieved by using the systems. This might include:

  - making suggestions in the suggestion scheme

  - raising questions at presentations or meetings

  - contributing to a task force, quality team or virtual team

  - speaking or writing directly to a more senior manager expressing an idea or concern.

Probably the most important element in encouraging upward communication is your attitude.

- make time to hear the individual out. While you always have other things to do, the issue an individual raises may be extremely important to the service your department offers its customers. Your job as a manager is to make sure that you do this as well as possible; the idea might just make the difference. In effect, if you don't find the time to listen to the person, you are telling them that you alone are the person in the department who has good ideas, which is a significant demotivator;

- really listen to what he or she has to say. Don't presume you know what they will say before they have had a chance to say it. (see Chapter 9 on effective listening);

- try not to be defensive. It may seem to you that the issue being raised is an implicit or explicit attack on the way you run the department or of "management" in general in the organisation of which you are a part. Any hint of defensiveness on your part will put people off coming to you again and the channels of communication will become blocked. Try to see the issue from their point of view;

- if an issue is raised in a team meeting, protect the person mentioning the problem or idea from the ridicule or cynicism of the rest of the team. If appropriate, offer to discuss it with the person outside the meeting. People will quickly pick up whether or not you appear to value ideas raised by people in the team; taking **all** ideas seriously sends signals that you value everyone's contribution.

TAKING ACTION

If the issue is within your capability to judge, but for one reason or another you decide to take no action on the idea your reasons need to be explained fully, in many cases to the whole team, as well as to the individual who raised the issue.

If the reasons are **not** clearly communicated people will presume that you are simply not interested or cannot be bothered, and will themselves cease to bother to tell you their ideas or problems. However good your reasons, you may not convince the individual who raised the issue, and he or she may complain to other people in the team. You need to convince the **whole** team of the reasons for taking no action.

THE LINE MANAGER'S ROLE

If you cannot address the issue yourself, you are
responsible for making sure it reaches the attention of
those who can. How exactly this is done will depend
on the systems and culture of your organisation. It may
be that your team member can simply send a memo or
mention the issue to the relevant person themselves. If this
is the case, your only role is to make sure that your team
member knows who is the right person to address.

It may be, however, that the communication has to
come through you. This can be awkward if you disagree
with the point raised or if it is critical of you. You do,
however, have an obligation to your team member and to
the organisation to pass it on.

Where managers become filters of bad news the
organisation builds up problems. It is less likely that
team members will come to you again with problems
or ideas; it is, of course, just possible that an idea that
seems loopy to you is actually a major opportunity for the
organisation.

Don't endorse an idea if you disagree with it. You do
need, however, to press for a full reply even if the idea is
not to be adopted, so that you can demonstrate to your
team member that the idea has been properly examined
seriously by those qualified to judge it.

BIBLIOGRAPHY

A Briefer's Guide to Team Briefing
Patrick Wintour (The Industrial Society, rev. 1989)

Team Briefing Information Pack
(The Industrial Society 1992)

The Effective Communicator
John Adair (The Industrial Society 1988)

The Right Report
Alan Barker (The Industrial Society 1993)

Letters at Work
Alan Barker (The Industrial Society 1993)

Pocket Guide to Written English
Michael Temple (John Murray rev. 1992)

Communication Skills: A Practical Handbook
Edited by Chrissie Wright (The Industrial Society 1993)